Rockpool Rap

RODERICK HUNT

Pictures by Ben Cort

Oxford University Press
1997

In a small and sheltered rockpool,
on a beach down by the sea,
lived the limpet, crab, and starfish,
and the sea anemone.

Now in that sheltered rockpool
lived a clever clam called Clive.
He was very good at singing—
you should see him jump and jive.

Love my job,
jump and bob.
Join the jumping shellfish jive.
Fast and slow,
high and low.
Oh, it's good to be alive!

Clive was very good at singing,
and he played a big guitar.
So he changed his name to Elvis,
and became a big rock star.

Love my job,
jump and bob.
Join the jumping shellfish jive.
Fast and slow,
high and low.
Oh, it's good to be alive!

7

When Elvis gave a concert,
how his fans would scream and sob!
All the barnacles would sigh, sigh, sigh,
and limpet hearts would throb.

"What do you know,
it's my show,
take your places in the row.
Big and small...room for all.
Come, you shellfish
short and tall!"

9

But Elvis grew too famous,
and he cried, "I've heard the call.
I'm a star, and I'll go far.
Now this rockpool's far too small."

Fans cried "Cool!
He's no fool!
And his fame is sure to grow.
He's a star,
he'll go far!
He's a superstar, you know."

He waited till a wave rolled in.
His fans watched from below.
Then Elvis floated from the pool,
and sailed out with the flow.

Fans cried "Cool!
He's no fool!
And his fame is sure to grow.
He's a star,
he'll go far!
He's a superstar you know."

But he didn't find the open sea
a happy place at all.
The open sea was not to be
a friendly concert hall.

"What do you know,
it's my show,
take your places in the row.
Big and small...room for all.
Come, you seafish
short and tall!"

Elvis danced and he sang,
and he played his big guitar.
He rocked and rolled and rattled,
and he shouted, "I'm a star!"

Love my job,
jump and bob.
Join the jumping seafish jive.
Fast and slow,
high and low.
Oh, it's good to be alive!

But electric eel and stingray
circled all around the show.
The hungry sharks swam up above,
and swordfish swam below.

Sharkfish slide,
sharkfish glide,
sharkfish circled mean and slow.
Electric eel made Elvis feel
it was time to stop the show.

All the big fish laughed and teased him,
when poor Elvis sang a song.
They said, "Scram! You're just a clam!
You get back where you belong!"

SCRAM!

Sharkfish slide...sharkfish glide,
sharkfish circled mean
and slow.
Electric eel...made Elvis feel
it was time to stop the show.

The sea grew dark and stormy.
Elvis cried, "I've been a fool!
The open sea's no place for me,
I must go back to my pool."

Big wave crash,
big wave bash,
in a whoosh, whoosh, whooshy squall.
"The stormy sea is not for me.
I don't like it here at all!"

Elvis went back to his rockpool,
with his suitcase and guitar.
"I've been a fool, it's in this pool—
and not at sea—that I'm a star."